4/22

Gallery Books
Editor: Peter Fallon

WHAT THE HAMMER

Dermot Healy

WHAT THE HAMMER

Gallery Books

What the Hammer
is first published
simultaneously in paperback
and in a clothbound edition
in August 1998.

The Gallery Press
Loughcrew
Oldcastle
County Meath
Ireland

ISBN 1 85235 222 1 *(paperback)*
     1 85235 223 X *(clothbound)*

The Gallery Press acknowledges the financial assistance
of An Chomhairle Ealaíon / The Arts Council, Ireland,
and the Arts Council of Northern Ireland.

Contents

What the hammer? what the chain?
In what furnace was thy brain?
What the anvil? what dread grasp
Dare its deadly terrors clasp?

– from 'The Tyger',
William Blake

Sea-sand

The splash grows closer
till it's like someone
turning in the bed
beside you.

The waves know their way
intimately; they arrive
like neighbours, closing
gates after them,

filling in all the gaps
in the walls, the silences,
whatever misunderstandings
may have arisen

since the last time
this great big water for which
there's no metaphor
came pounding over the bar.

As the tide gathers
the grains of sand
that cemented the stones that built the house
begin to stir.

They want to be down there
where they came from,
among all that wild
phosphorescence.

Slowly they slip through
the ears of wheat, the bog-soil,
the manure and soot and frog-spit
that plug the rocks

till at full tide the walls weep.
The walls run.
The house shifts.
Tear-ducts appear on the eaves.

Clusters of sparks
light up the bog:
the curlew hails you.
The sea-sand rains.

It seems ages
since you've had
whoever this is
in your arms.

The Serenities

for Helen

A fire lit.
Candles burning.
The animals in.

The last weather report
giving warm breezes
from the south.

Our lovemaking sweet
and, just before sleep,
thoughts like prayer.

Then the dark
where, when you turn,
I turn,

as if we were
for one beautiful moment
looking the same way

from some height
at something moving slowly
out of sight.

June

1

A summer storm comes riding over the waves
like a pirate

and, anchoring to nothingness,
raises a flag of spume some sixty foot high

beyond the sheer drop
in case we'd forget.

2

Salt rains down on the cabbages.
Snails turn to spit.

The waves lift
rocks in silence,

like convicts who have been
condemned to this.

3

White butterflies dart round in the sun
    among the beach stones.
The beach keels.

With a great maw
the land empties itself

into the sea.

Sea-fire

It catches on calm days
away out on the Atlantic;
just a small flame

racing inland.
The billows smoke
each side of the boat

and a school of mackerel sparkle.
Waves send up stars.
The roar of flames is steady.

Sea-fire!
At the edge of an oar
beyond the lead-line of the net.

Inishmurray is going up!
And all beyond Inishmurray!
And at the alt

white ash comes in with the tide.
Air thickens with salt.
Between here and Mayo

the sea has been torched.
Soot strikes the lava.
A long time

before the cold blue stretches out
and the moon cools
in the white swell.

Sea-fire! Even the words would do
if there never was that leap of light
beyond the dripping net.

Rust

The wind seeds the air with salt
and, like weeds,

all bad news,
rust spreads fast,

snapping the handles off cars,
and cracking the heads of spades.

Hinges give
and doors fall open

suddenly, in the middle of the night;
then enter the mermen

with bags of winkles
they've been collecting

since before Christ.

Coal Bags

The half-empty bags of Polish coal
blow in a July wind
like monks' cowls.

On a cold winter evening
this ceremony
goes on for hours

in what was the cart shed.
The monks go.
Now it's the turn of the nuns.

July Storm

1

For three days the sea blooms
in every crevice.

Ever nurturing,
always rampant,

it rains down on the porch;
and seeds burst open in the haggard.

For three days the three rooms are full of light
and disturbance.

Sea-weed sneezes.
The sand ticks.

The loll and the loop,
the hula-hoop.

On the first day the wash. The bellows.
The guru. The goose.

The moon swings like a lamp
in the hands of a madman.

On the second day the prow of Bulben
goes under.

Suds land on the roof
quietly, like bog cotton,

and waves fill
with wave blossom.

On the third day the peopleless world
starts speaking.

The word for beach
rings true. The word for gull.

The *S* in sea rows out to *E*.
The *O* in ocean soars.

Gravel and shingle
do an *Excuse Me*.

The pounding. The cooing.
The slap. The shriek!

She encroaches upon the winded house
with sea-thrift.

Then turns away across a bed
of sighing shale.

2
Next morning
let the old land rest.

Move the wrong stone,
the ocean pours in.

Death, the Cat

Death came in the door like a cat
and stood and sniffed the room I was in.

It sat there on the threshold for a second
while I looked to where the animal should be.

Its smell raced towards me,
the smell of rain on dry stone,

water not far off, wet fur, a hot breath,
and eyes that your eyes cannot see

settling on you for an instant.
Then the cat withdrew silently

with the smell last of all to go.
I put my head against the bedstead

and knew that death had visited.
It frightened me.

I saw myself from the cat's point of view,
a man in bed who is not sleeping,

happy in a way, distracted, a sinner,
aware that it will not go forever

and, for a moment, deeply afraid.
It pitied me, that cat.

It pitied me as I turned my mind to other things
and began to think of finishing the wall on the beach.

I counted the number of books I needed to write
before I'd feel worthwhile.

I thought of those I'd known who've died.
Soon I was down on the actual beach

building a wall I knew would be taken away
in a January storm.

At this work I am content.
It eases me. I smoke a fag, look out to sea,

and I think with wonder –
the day the cat crosses the threshold

all of this I see and feel will be someone else's.
The barnacle geese, the wagtails,

not only Inishmurray, but Ardbollan,
the stretch of sea from here to Bundoran.

Someone else, not I, will lie awake at night
and sleep with a radio on,

or watch with amazement
at first light a beach full of enchanted hares.

And with a sort of relief
I suddenly realise

even the cat will be his.

Joe Donlon

I stand in the doorway
like Joe Donlon before me,

hunched-up huge
in the candlelight on the stones,

looking at the broad black theatre
of the inland night:

only two blooms in my garden –
the moon-white pool of flood water

in the bog, and the quiet race
from the bog to the beach.

The dog lands a stick at my feet.
Throw it! Throw it! he says.

I throw it as far as I can
and he disappears

towards the sound
of its fall in the grass.

A long time he's searching out there
in the dark.

Then he lands it again at my feet
without a sound, without a bark.

We seem then to flounder,
the dog and the house and myself,

towards what I cannot name.
We move a little across the street,

down darkness,
by sheds, through grief,

in this strange place
where the vastness closes in

as it must have, on certain nights,
round Joe Donlon.

What the Hammer

EARTH

The daffodil is sinning,
the potato drill is sinning.

Think of the sins of the worm
as it slips through the dab,

the deep blue dab;
the beautiful sins of the roots under the maple;

flint, frog, lime,
shoots, shale, the divine

moist smell that wets
the throat in October.

The spade sins. The shovel.
The pick.

The field in winter. The mountain.
The hayrick.

The ashpit.
To sin is to be

the cabbage, the turnip,
the pansy, the sweet-grass,

the seed of the hollyhock.
To sin is to exist

at all. To draw breath
above earth.

To have dug in manure
to feed the rose.

To have seen the orange peel
rotting under the cypress tree.

AIR

The first time it was
like a snipe of stout,

straight up through the nostrils
and right out

the top of the head.
The clean lung

like a bell.
The note going through the accordion.

The whistle in the throat.
Air of travellers,

air of climbers,
Seamus Ennis's song,

James Coyle's lament,
the smoker's cough,

the tiny breath of a leaf
shaking

through the rushes.
Don't forget the rushes,

don't forget the reeds,
don't forget the fingerholes,

the mouth-piece,
the drone,

the wind from the north-west
in perfect pitch

against the gable,
the groan of the rafter

just after
daybreak.

FIRE

Ivy smells good,
the cherry better,

the larch is happy in flames,
but best of all is

the apple branch
when it's burning.

And don't forget the turf –
one sod would be enough,

crisp, dried, frosted,
taking with a whoosh of sparks

in the dark.
Tap the bark of the elm

and you'll hear the leap of the spark
just before

the flames take.
Kill a Viking

on St John's eve.
Watch fields of wheat

go up in a sunrise.
Smoke from afar tells us

we're not here alone.
The fish spits its scales,

the hair of the pig
dries and cracks,

and a burning horseshoe
stamps home.

WATER

It grows still as perfume,
becomes lakes

and rainbows;
breaks loud overhead

and moves towards
what you'll forget

till the time
comes round again.

It has no shoes,
goes barefoot

into dreams
and nightmares.

It gave us
tails and feet

and wings.
Tide-maker,

hoarder of salts,
thirst-maker,

stiff mirage by the pier,
you haunt the rocky bar

with danger.
I hear your snipes,

your seagulls.
I hear your moan

on winter nights
beneath my bed.

You fall as light.
You turn holy.

I've seen you lift the splashing
rocks without a sound.

Signs

When the moon begins
filling in
that's a sign.

The gall-bow
is a sure sign.

So is the ring.

Sea-spray

It sends up blooms
that scatter seed
across the fields;

its shoots
are on the crest
of every wave;

sea-spray,
the unalterable
ever-there!

Rootless, fresh-smelling,
it lives for a second
in a sweep of froth

that chalks
the banging rocks
of Ardbollan

with a thin line of salt.
Mermen wear it
in their hair

and seamen gather wreaths
from off their boats
of finest

sea-spray. They are
gathering it now,
somewhere.

Pity the Moon!

The moon on the rocks
has hunkered down
like an old man.

He sits where the sea leaps
and looks at the reflection
of his face.

If the water is coming in
his face will be large and lovely.
If the water is going out

his face narrows with sadness.
Pity the old moon
at the edge of the rock!

He is filled
with sentiment and wine
and must not stay here.

Not a moment longer!
So he brings a hand over his face
and becomes

a light chasing
through the depths
till all that is left

is the eye of a frightened foal
beseeching us below
the green frond of a wave.

The Slip of a Moon

It's a moon
you could hang your hat on
or peg a clothesline to.

It's a domestic moon.
Bring it indoors
and hang it in the wardrobe

and you could drape
the black dress or the blue
from its thin sloped shoulders.

It's an anchor
come free in the fast-flowing sea
of nothingness.

It's the anchor
that holds us fast
to what there is.

August

Puffs of rain
strike the dry rocks

like spit;
then burst open.

The sand-flies
gather like bees

and hop. The sea-weed
ticks, ticks.

The olearia leaf stirs in the wind
to the sound of the paw of a dog

striking gravel.
The clams are clicking

in their bucket.
A travel shop

of sea-shells
and fossils

arrives through the riddle.
A sighing cow

looks towards home.
The field fills with coughs.

Everything is on the go.
Time is moving inland.

Other Signs

The sound of a car door slamming
means she's from the West.

Gunshots and she's
angry.

A tobacco spit in the sand
marks the razor fish.

Colours

You'd be surprised
how black black is
when it's blue with rain.

And what do you do with the light
that comes in off the sea?
You might as well

forget what you look like
before you could ever begin
walking in it.

September

The greatest high-tide,
the happiest birds,
and the drunk on the road
who has been hurt in love.

The Armada at Streedagh

Out to sea
there is the snap of a castanet.

Boats are going down
to the tune of the bolero.

Sovereigns are sifted
by old storms.

A bull, bleeding profusely,
makes for Grange.

A Dream

I had a dream
in which Jimmy Foley died
in the back room.

I lived out towards the front
oblivious of his hunger
for days and days.

And when they said
'But he's in your house!'
I didn't believe them.

I started to explain
but my voice grew distant
and eerie.

My anxiety was choking me
that I could have been such a fool
to let Jimmy die in my own house.

Imagine my relief on wakening!
To see the light still burning
in his window.

And then I thought of my mother
who had forgotten to feed her sister,
with Maisie sitting diligently in her room

afraid to walk for fear of falling.
And when I pushed open the door and asked her,
'Have you not eaten yet?'

she said, 'It's alright. Someone will come.'
Her faith shy and absolute.
Then mother remembers.

Soon everyone is running to feed Maisie.
And maybe that is why I dreamed
Jimmy dead.

In the world of dream
where anxiety can never be appeased
everyone has someone dying of hunger.

Loneliness

I'm never lonely,
said Jimmy Foley,

I know that I'm here,
that's all.

I might sit up till two
or three, happily.

Lie down,
get up again.

A couple of hours
on my back

will do.
Lonely? No.

There's enough
in my head

to do me
for a while longer.

After that
who knows?

The Prayer

for Noel Kilgallon

When Peggy was dying
her son leaned over to whisper
the Our Father into her ear.

She opened her eyes.
'Things must be bad,' she said,
'that you've started praying.'

The Wren Girl

When you pressed on the eyelids
you kept in all she saw

for us to see in our time.
When you wrapped the skull

in a scarf you sent
her off to school again.

Be careful with the lips,
for everything she ever said

is going through our heads.
And for old times' sake

let in the wren girl
on the doorstep.

It's time to bury the dead.

A Funeral

in memory of Jimmy Foley

Twelve shovels
dug the grave;

the same twelve
fill it in.

It takes the length
of a rosary.

All together
tap the dab,

kick muck
off a heel,

toss old bones
into a bag.

The shovels
work like oars

rowing the dead man
from this world

to the next.
Then the lights

go back
to the West.

Travelling

1

When the eye lights on water
and you say the word *Shannon*

to yourself, the spirits soar
and the soul is cheered,

as the train flies over the early winter-blue
of that long moving river

with an audacious roar.
Then time stands still.

In the short span of the bridge
from East to West,

the senses fill
with other words for water.

The body is seeped.
The brain teems.

I'm back on the bank of a river
I've not stood on in ages,

and there's nearly too much to remember
and there's not too far to go.

Then with a loud scream
it's over.

The train kicks sideways
onto land. We speed towards Sligo

through the drenched green
of mid-November.

2
A light in the dark
carried steadily up a further ridge

like the light in the corner of the eye
astronauts have when they come home

from all those days and nights watching the earth
swing like a lamp below them.

The Old Chiefs

Not till I'd seen
the old chiefs

trying to land their boats
out of the world of myth

did I hear the wheatear
and the finch.

Approaching Car

Many times I've looked up
or run to the window
to see who was coming.

And who was it?
The rain from the south-west
driving past

in a squall
with no lights on
except the one

you see at dead of night
inside a car
on a stranger's face

as he speeds by your place
in the direction
all strangers go.

The Wandering Cat

If you find your cat
wandering far from home

don't lift him!
He'll weigh so heavy

he'll never leave your hands.

My House is Tiny

My house is tiny
and my sorrow
is the smallest
at this end of the country.

And yet the whole sea
at my back
can fit into
the most frightened

human mind.

The Cuckoo-pint in a Commonage in Ennis

for Jean and Bernard

1

Among the bluebells,
this torrid plant –

the cuckoo-pint;
a dark pod with its foreskin folded neatly

inside a tall curved leaf.
A dusky shoot on a stem

in a wrap of foliage.
Intimate and exotic,

this gentleman and lady.
He is perfect, youthful, soot-tipped;

she stretches round him like a wing.
It is not her first time.

Beads are forming on her lip.
The leaf grows moist.

2

He is a Negroid dancer
standing on his toe

in a music-box.
She holds a fan

across her face.
They have just finished a step

across the forest floor.
She has let him go

and is opening wide.
He, with a perfect leap,

has landed inside.

3
The music for the coupling
is the puffball,

the silent scattering
of clocks,

and the plant-hush –
quietest of all breaths.

The No-tree

Sometimes the moon
gets caught in the high branches
of the No-tree,

and you have to shake
and shake the No-tree
to set it free.

Even this may never be enough.

Light

Each scrap of daylight
that crosses the sill
is a black page
which I must fill.

Fire

in memory of Aidan

If you let the fire die
the soul scurries across the field
like a burning coal
off to another hearth.

Oh disloyal soul
separated from me
in my cold house!

Cormorants

They fly over like flagships of the devil
with messages between the dead.

Fighting to keep a straight line
they bring news to Ulysses,

then back again to Lethe
with his letters for the boatman.

Only the cormorant is allowed into hell.
That's why he stands with his wings out

on an unsheltered rock
imploring the heavens

to forgive him for all
that he's seen and heard.

The Litany of the Wagtail

Chirp of the flirt,
scurry through the blur,
sudden snatch of song.

Pulse gatherer.
Time keeper.

Sidestep of the polka,
tig on the street,
marionette of the wind.

Altar-boy's curtsy,
white thread of tweed.

Ceaseless diving-rod.

Warrior of the mirror.
Noon trill.
The cry from beyond the sickbed.

Groom of sweet wooing,
morning tuning-fork,
skiff of the field.

Breast of the hailstone.
Nib dipped in clear ink.

Strike of the dandelion clock,
bounce of brightness,
chase down-the-wind.

Rosary of shingle,
loyal chime of winter,
quill of the rain-bead.

Welcome eye on the sea-wall,
slim reed of willow,
bib of black silk.

Sheath of wings,
needle of the spinning compass,
fast dart past the cold horse.

Rain baton.
Cry above the gunshot of the sea.

Joyful alarm beyond the gable,
companion of the short day.

Quick skip of the heart,
glad bell at storm's end.

The White Road from Aghadoon

Bawling lambs
and water chattering
like water-birds.

The sneeze of a grasshopper.
My shadow on the white road
ahead of me

with jacket tongs dangling.
Everywhere marvellous alarms;
jingles, whistles,

cave cries.
The stones are singing
in the blue hole.

Eyes

The strange thing is
that from you were a babe
the size of your eyes
never changes.

The colour of the pupils may
but the orb through which we see
is determined
in the cradle.

The difference is that
what looked huge at first
comes smaller,
and what

mattered not at all in what you saw
grows large.
It's only the eyes
remain the same.

Only the eyes.

Wrongs

In the other world
they might have
laws and rules, too,
or maybe
none

but at least in this one
we must not patronise
the drunk,
having once
been drunk,

or the sober,
a state we well might be
sometime, sober,
knowing the discipline
is work,

sleep, not to get
up before yourself,
sleep, nor to go
to sleep
before yourself,

and yes to feel begrudgery,
jealousy,
as a lesson
that teaches
humility.

And do not ask
for just one more.
The juke-box is full
of our songs.
And whether

we can sing them
or not makes
no difference. The world
knows
our wrongs.

The Barnacles

A string of pearls
worn just before dusk,

the writing in the sky
with wing tip,

a long dappling
and the chatter

of a flight of archangels,
a shifting grain of sand

honking inland.
Birds that never yield,

the geese, just after daybreak,
going to the goose field.

Raining in Georgia

1

In a pool near the bar
the sea-urchins do
a pin dance.

2

How do I know you've been looking
at your face? The half cup of tea gone cold
at the foot of the mirror.

3

How do I know when I'm sick?
When the air outside rises
like a full tide

against the window sill.
When there is a murmuring
that should not be there,
it's time.

4

In the hall the wedding guests
stopped to listen
to the bray of an ass.

5

Take off your coat –
it's raining in Georgia.

Footsteps

I heard a footstep outside
of someone coming home late

or heading out early.
Of course that cannot be –

the road ends at the pier of the gate,
but that sound

of something thrown
from Ardbollan

brought back all
those footfalls:

the step of some West Indian
skipping through Brixton

or party-goer tramping
down Leinster Road.

Like a metronome
in the far distance

they pick their beat home;
then draw near,

till underneath
they grow loud;

for a moment
they're in the room,

and their forms
ghost across the ceiling,

then fall away;
a shadow-army

in retreat.
I've heard the marching steps

of soldiers in Quito,
Orangemen on the Ravenhill,

Italians in Pimlico,
skinheads in Sligo,

all approach and recede
down streets

that went by my door.
There was the sound of radios,

argument, cars,
lovers in different languages

speaking in different bars –
hatred in a crass loud voice,

defiance,
the soft sound of blood,

whispers, curses,
dogs;

and always, last thing at night
or first thing in the morning,

this lone step.
Like the swift clip of the baker

going down Main Street
just before six:

mathematically correct;
a man you could set your clock by.

Someone who knows where he is going
or coming from,

a pivot between certainties
in the small hours.

But now all those steps
have stopped

just short of Culimney.
Only fishermen and divers

or spirits and birds
make the trek

to the alt and, yet,
this lone step out of the past

has reached me.
Just when I thought

the procession of strangers
past my door had ended

an old friend I've never met
has come to call.

It could be anybody.
The monk in Crete

slapping along in his sandals
to early Mass,

the thump of feet
last thing down Bridge Street.

And although it might be
a plank flipped across the yard

or something else
of inconsequence,

oh it will always be
the plainsong

of the ordinary
that reduces whole cities out there

to a step
on a street

and contains them all,
all those footfalls.

The Tern of the Mullet

The warbler
has a tic
of lifting
her wings
to emphasise
certain notes.

Have you got that, the warbler asks,
that note on mortality?

Yes, the tern
cries, and her
shriek echoes
back and forth
through the windless
inlet.

Yes! Yes! Yes!
answers the tern of the Mullet.

Acknowledgements

Acknowledgement is due to the editors of *Force 10* and *Poetry Now Anthology* (Dún Laoghaire/Rathdown) in which some of these poems were published.

'What the Hammer' and 'The Litany of the Wagtail' were premièred and broadcast in a musical composition by Michael Holohan on AART Radio in IMMA on 11 October 1994 and subsequently performed in the Droichead Arts Centre on 7 December 1994.